The Taxing of Ke'sha Dennis
One Woman's Journey Embracing Serenity, Self, and Spirit

MAWMedia Group
Reno NV

Publisher: MAWMedia Group

First Edition: July 2019

The Taxing of Ke'sha Dennis: One Woman's Journey Embracing Serenity, Self, and Spirit / By Ke'sha Dennis

ISBN: 978-1-943616-07-7

MAWMedia Group, LLC
3095 Fairwood Dr
Reno, NV 89502

www.mawmedia.com

Acknowledgements

Thank you to everyone I've crossed paths with in this journey called life. To my beautiful daughters, thanks for loving mommy. To my love and bossy silent business partner. To those who've attempted to hurt me, I thank you for allowing me to turn your pain into my triumph! To those that have told me the truth, no matter how hard it was. To everyone helping my vision come to life, thanks for your time and dedication. To my family, good, bad, or indifferent, I love you. God bless everyone, and thank you for allowing me to share my journey.

Dedication

For my grandmother, Roberta Greene

The Taxing of Ke'sha Dennis

Contents

Ke'sha Dennis

Section I: Family Seeds

Chapter 1: Great Grandmother

I'm the type of person that needs an explanation. I want clarification. I want the what, when, where, who, how, and why. If one piece is missing, I turn two years old. It feels like a slow person moment. It may be something someone else would overlook, but I can't continue until those questions are answered. I am also a person who enjoys puzzles. I enjoy making connections and communicating with my own brand of mystery and wisdom. I am more spiritual than religious, more positive than negative, more progress than backsliding, and more do than talk about it. I am a wonderful woman, a wonder-woman that has paid her dues.

Being in that space of super humanity allows me to grow and reach new people. I want God to allow his light to shine through me so that I can meet other lights. We can then move as one big light. The more people I can touch, the more people can connect and see their opportunities. I need everyone to reach their breakthrough. Light, to me is peaceful. The first person that I've ever heard speak of connecting to light is another June-born, Kanye West. I heard him talk about light. There is energy in light. I've always felt a sense of peace in low light — a clean source of energy, illuminating. Everything about light is positive and peaceful.

I have always run from negative and mean energy. If the negative energy sparks or draws it out of me, I felt out of control. I would rather not be around those type of people. I am never afraid of the other person. I am afraid of any darkness they provoked within me. God's consequences always made me walk away before I got myself into trouble.

No person exemplified light more than my great-grandmother. Her energy was a glow. The softness of her hair, glow of her skin, flaws and all, she was perfect. I never saw her degrade anyone or belittle others. She was sophisticated. I never saw bad or negative energy from her. I was drawn to unique and intelligent souls, because of her.

My great-grandmother planted the seed of determination within me. She was born in 1917. She was one of the smartest women I've ever known. She knew something about every topic. She fed me both physically and intellectually. I am a thinker and need constant brain stimulation. I always felt the need to learn. I craved it. I would love to sit at the edge of her bed and just listen. Something brilliant was certain to come out. She was going to make me think. Whether it was solving a puzzle on Wheel of Fortune or answering a question on Jeopardy, she always inspired my thoughts. I used to sit on her bed and watch her do crossword puzzles for hours captivated at her command of language and her knowledge of words.

I need to be in a position where my brain is stimulated. While other kids were outside exercising their bodies, I was inside exercising my brain. It was natural for me to learn from observation. I studied things people did and things that they said. People were intriguing to me. Especially smart people. Older women had a comforting feature to them. I always felt comforted and loved when around them. They were always concerned about how I was and how I was being taken care of. I was attracted to my great-grandma's energy. I didn't see any wrong in her. I always wanted to make her happy. She was an angel. She was my angel.

We would play Scrabble. She would make me look up words in the dictionary. It made me want to be smart. It was a challenge I wanted to achieve. I wanted to win. Not too many people in the family could win playing against my great-grandma in scrabble, but I finally did when I was 8. I have always wondered whether she allowed me to win because it took me seven years to win her again. I will always wonder, but I am proud of it nonetheless. I never beat her in a crossword puzzle though. I soon gave up on that.

I played cards with the adults at 7 years old. I would cook my great-grandma eggs, and she would make mayonnaise and fried egg sandwich. She liked that I knew how to make the perfect over medium egg. She was in her mid to late 60s and was facing the deterioration of aging. She had bad knees. I took pride in taking care of her, including emptying her bucket. It bothered me that her bucket would get so full of urine and feces. Even though she had other grandchildren living with her older than me, they didn't seem as eager to help. This is what made me believe I wanted to be a registered nurse, because I wanted to be there when people needed someone the most.

Her Light & My Mission

It is my great-grandmother's light that, at least in part, guides who I am becoming today. I am at a point in my life where I am remembering that before kids and any man, there was Ke'sha. Now, I'm on a mission. Harriet Tubman is my role model. I have always thought of myself as Harriet. Maybe it's, because my birthday is Juneteenth; the day President Lincoln freed the slaves.

I love the fact that she was kind of gangster. She reminded me of older women back in the day, because she had a helping spirit. She was a selfless leader, wanting her people to experience freedom. She kept it together and made sure her traveling students were focused and educated for the mission. I wonder if the determination of making it to freedom is what made her successful every trip. I read about how she would threaten people that were tempted to turn back. She would say that she would off them rather than risk the whole group. That would be me.

Ke'sha Dennis

Before now, I would always sacrifice to my detriment; I would feed my money and energy into someone else to win. I never looked at myself as an option. My flaw had always been that I would not ask for help. I was a very independent child. I loved to feed all the neighborhood kids and do their hair. Making everyone around me feel pretty and happy has always been fun to me.

During that time, I got closer to God. I was kicked out of my home because the landlord wanted a rent increase. I had four of my five daughters that still depended on me. I was sleeping in hotels and on my cousin's floor.

I am grateful that I had a place to stay, but this was not the life I desired. The revelation was that I could never allow myself to be in that place again. I had always gone out of my way to make everyone comfortable. I had to realize that everyone isn't going to do for you what you did for them. It was thrust into my face. God's message!

I must acknowledge Gina, who showed up during that time. She was one friend who came through for me in a pinch. "I have a house full of kids and two dogs," she said, "but you are welcome to stay." It didn't work because her place was too far from my job. Just for her to offer was grand. I knew she was genuine. I felt it.

I was ready to allow all my household possessions to be taken away. My friend Jolene saved me from that fate. I had only known her for three years. She told me, "Ke'sha, you are not going out like that." She called Starving Students, a campus program for students who fall on hard times. They took my possessions to a storage unit. I call these two my forever friends. My daycare provider/Godmother Sarah, Aunt Margaret, and Auntie Tonie helped some, but there's nothing like having your own. You don't realize the importance of having your own until you lose it.

I accepted that money was always coming to me, and things were going to work out. I was tripping over the people that were hurting around me. Then, a time came when I was in need, and I had barely had anyone. I realized that I was betting on the wrong people. I have decided to put myself first. I began to realize that help could be given in more ways than nursing. Financial literacy and business became important to me eventually. But God was not finished educating me about the world.

I realized that many people fed off drama because they were so enmeshed and co-dependent in worldly things. I witnessed examples in many places. I was unclear at the time how the light I so enjoyed from my great grandmother could play in this world coexisting with the need prioritize self. I now know that the answer begins with choice. I don't have any room anymore for people that sit in their misfortune. I firmly believe we are all capable of changing our situation.

I learned to stop talking and to focus on those ready and willing to learn skill sets that will advance them in life. Cutting people off is me informing them that they are not respecting me, and I no longer invite their energy into my space. I used to feel like God would punish me because I didn't forgive them 7200 times 7. I realized that not allowing toxic people in your space is warranted and needed for progression. I am aware that God doesn't punish people for forgiving from a distance. There's nothing in the word that says God wants you to place yourself around those out to hurt you.

Financial Help

I have noticed that finances are the problem in many people's lives. There should not be a correlation between happiness and money. People should go on a path to discover themselves and find love for themselves. When you find your purpose, it will become your passion. Once your passion helps and serves others, the money will come. I approach money the way I do because I know that investing in me is never money lost.

I am on a mission to make as many of my people millionaires. We deserve a life that provides true freedom. God has given me a gift to help free people from their burdens. Some people simply need to know someone else sees their gifts. God gave me the ability to help others' visions come to life by helping them establish a business and helping them realize their gifts. There's a lot of people who need to see people from similar backgrounds doing what they've dreamed of for themselves. This provides a sense of motivation, and the vision can now be brought to life.

I want to gear people up and get them financially educated so that they can live a life of financial freedom. Financial strain is like having on shackles, with a noose on and only your big toe holding you on the chair. If you slip, it's over. No one should ever have to live like that. I am learning as much about finances to create a different pattern. I want us to live like kings and queens. With the appropriate financial education, we can get there.

We have never been taught anything by anyone. It's unfortunate, but if they did it to Yeshua; they'll do it to his people. We didn't know what we needed to do, because the agenda was for us not to. The people that got to a certain level didn't want to or know how to help. If they came to help, they were being penalized. You must get knee-deep into the community if you really want to help. If you just give the money, the money is not reaching the people. You must get into it. If you do what you are supposed to do by organizing and executing a plan, a change would happen.

When you are given an empty pitcher without a water supply, you're left to fight to survive and figure things out quickly. My family didn't have inheritances or generational wealth. We had to start from the bottom of the food chain like many families in my neighborhood. I thought it was selfishness to bet on me. I thought I was here to be nice, helpful and serve God. I didn't know what my purpose was. I didn't know that I was here to shine and meet other lights. I wasn't looking at my own feelings. I wasn't happy because no matter what I did, no one around me ever seemed happy. I realized my pitcher was empty because I hadn't filled it. The issue wasn't that I couldn't make everyone else happy. The real issue was that I hadn't realized I needed to make

The Taxing of Ke'sha Dennis

myself happy first, before I could spread the love. I accomplished finding happiness and peace from within. God's love is real, and that love comes from within.

Ke'sha Dennis

Chapter 2: The Secret

Hebrews to Negros

I watched a film entitled *Hebrews to Negroes: Wake Up Black America*. It tells the ethnicity of the children of Israel through DNA research for a non-disputed scientific connection of the bible and Black people. After watching it, I remembered questioning several things that were answered in the video. I was a student in an African-Studies department when I attended Berkeley High School. It felt like being in college even while in high school. Those who hung out in the slopes, B building, or C building had so much fun. We had rap cyphers, water balloon fights, and tons of spirit-week pranks. The pot smokers were in the park across the street. I learned West African dance. I learned about how my people were kings and queens. I learned how men and women were to treat each other. I don't know where the disconnect occurred, but it came full circle when I got into the real world.

People didn't seem to get it on my level. I was hurting relationships because the truth can appear degrading and ugly. I was thinking that I was being encouraging. I now understand that certain people don't get it. I thought they were playing. I now know that people learn differently. Everyone wasn't in gifted and talented education, chess club, and reading the encyclopedia during the summer. I felt like I had to dumb myself down at times. Where I come from, you don't get the same treatment when you're smart, so I'd act like I didn't know certain things. I believed I had to play a lesser role and hold back my intellect.

Now, it's not for me to care about your thoughts. I speak my results more freely. I am attracting my tribe to me. Things are changing because I am communicating. I did my work. I had to make the vision boards; I had to read the books and cry. I had to go talk through the therapy sessions to recognize myself in the mirror. I had to get the tools. I had to learn the skills needed to break years of patterns and pathologies.

Family

My relationship with my mom is different. For the earlier part of my life, my mom was like the "Leave it to Beaver" mom. She went to work and school. We would celebrate all the holidays that I now know are pagan. We did our homework. It was structured. My mother always took me to church. We went to bible study and Sunday School. I was always waiting on the music. I loved the music. It was a cultural thing. The seed was planted. She had left my dad and was a strong single mom.

She eventually connected with my aunt's, husband's brother. He was a man from Nebraska. She fell in love with him. He was just no good. He must've been beyond troubled because he was a mean-spirited person. He was mean to children and mean to my mom. He had a bad energy. I knew his fate wouldn't be good if he did not change his ways. As a child, I thought it was unacceptable for people to treat people unfairly. I believed God was going to punish bad people right away. I now feel that some of the things that I experienced made me determined to stand up for myself and others. I was determined not to allow myself to be in certain situations.

Church at that time was important for cultural foundation of a relationship with Yeshua. This is the foundation that kept me. I knew that I always had refuge. I remember one time my mother jumped up in church flinging her arms. She was crying and falling back in church. I was 6. I thought she was playing at first. I didn't know what was going

Ke'sha Dennis

on with her. It scared me. I wanted to understand what was going on in church and why I wasn't understanding.

My mom owned a yearly Bible for new believers, NLT version. She would call me every day for bible study together with my brother and aunt. We held bible study routinely. I was always intrigued. I would read and gain understanding, but the bible has been a struggle for me. The narratives are obviously tampered with, but the energy still resonates.

The 1990s hit, and things changed. I was 13 and became super independent. The roles in my household put me in a position to grow up more quickly than my classmates. I was driving at 13 years of age. We always had food, a nice house, and afterschool activities; however, drugs hit my neighborhood with abandon, and I was forced to grow up fast. I was 15 when I went home to an empty home. Imagine leaving your home for the weekend as a teenager and coming home to an empty house with your belongings in a single box. That's what drugs does to families, unfortunately.

At first, I thought my mom just didn't care. But I realized that she didn't have some of the attributes of a mom because her mom died when she was 11. This was in the late 1960s. It was a generation that was full of famous interactions and liaisons that were tales within our family. I will leave it there. She never had it modeled to her, but she did an amazing job in comparison to statistics. This made it easier to forgive her.

I asked my great-grandma once about how my grandmother passed. It was the only time that I saw the light of that beautiful woman dim a little. The whole family attacked me. "Why would you ask her that!? That was her only child!" It's unfortunate when family doesn't provide genealogical history. I believe everyone should know where they come from and the circumstances that got them where they are.

The Taxing of Ke'sha Dennis

One of the fondest memories shared between my mother and I was a pre-school puzzle experience. My mother came to school for a conference or some event that allowed her to sit and work through puzzles the teacher made available to us. My mother couldn't get them together. For whatever reason, they didn't fit for her. The teacher assured her that it wasn't a deficit she should fault herself for.

"Only Kesha can put those together." The teacher called me over and invited me to demonstrate my process. I put the puzzles together, and my mother marveled.

"Kesha can solve any problem!" That stuck with me as I continued through school and the rest of my life. I am a problem solver. More specifically, I am a puzzle solver.

Ada Wada was a Japanese teacher I had. I will never forget her name because she introduced herself as having a name that was spelled the same whether it was spelled backwards or forwards, a palindrome. Her name was the first puzzle she offered me. From that first day, she offered the class a Problem of the Week. I made it my mission to solve those problems. I was not always successful, but I gave them my all.

Miss Ada Wada did not lob softballs for the young students to hit home runs. The problems were difficult. She did not think that we would be able to solve many. I surprised her when I was able to figure them out. She would sit with me and ask how I solved them. I communicated how I saw and understood what was being asked in the problem. I dissected it. I put it together in different ways mentally and transferred my ideas onto paper. I followed the fit as if the problem was a puzzle.

Math was easy for me because of this. Puzzles and math go hand in hand with me. I am always interested in breaking things down and reconstructing them. Breaking them apart as an abstraction of the mind and putting it together with my hands is amazing for me. I will work and work until everyone is exhausted to figure out a problem. No matter how long it takes, I am committed to the solution.

My Rebirth

Rebirth is a beautiful time in a woman's life. My prayer now is that God allows me to be guided by the Holy Spirit in all I do. I lost myself in relationships, love, and my children. I lost myself in everything but me. I am now taking me back. I am not giving me away in that same way. We must be selfish at times in order to be available for others.

At 16, I was pregnant, and by 19, I had two kids and a husband with sickle cell disease. I lived that life for nine years until a split. I met someone who was fun, spontaneous and had energy. He was the opposite of my husband. I met a tall, dark handsome guy I could have fun with. I was happy to have someone that liked adventures as much as myself. He was the product of a drug-addicted mom and an absent father. I got pregnant by him, and that was the beginning of a major life-change.

Around the age of 25, I had some wild days. I didn't feel like I was treated right in the marriage. Turmoil ensued. I didn't know it was as serious as I do now. I had to find out a lot on my own. I had a lot of feelings misguided, unloved, wondering what I did wrong. No one was there to teach me anything about being in a relationship. I grew from a 15-year-old child, homeless into a married, adult with multiple children.

I know now that God was carrying me the entire time. I didn't really think about it. I would go back to church periodically. I remained in school majority of the time. Through all the unappreciation and abandonment, I saw an out through school. I rarely missed a day. My thirst for knowledge has always been unquenchable.

Chapter 3: The Dream

Wakeup Call

I was almost 18 or 18 years old when I had a dream that would pull me toward a greater connection with light and love. I don't remember whether I was pregnant or not, but I had one of my daughters at the time. I had completed Western Dental. I was a certified dental assistant.

I woke up from the dream. I remember burning blocks the size of buildings falling from the sky. They were just huge. I looked for people and none were found. I continued to move, hoping the blocks wouldn't crush me. Different scenes from my life flashed into memory as I ran. I looked up to dodge the falling, fire-blazing buildings and down to see them crash and burn on the ground. I was frightened. Another flash and I saw my brother in the distance jumping up and down and smiling.

"Jesus is coming!" My brother chanted. "We're about to go!"

"I don't know if I'm going," I responded, disappointed. I felt like I wasn't ready.

"That's not a good thing right now," he responded emotionless. I was a child who knew God, but I was not a reader of the bible. I went to church and I knew of God, but I didn't know him like I know him now. Life is much different when you truly know him. It was just before crack hit the streets. My mother had us in church so much during my childhood. Everyone knew the kids that went to church. Church was a second family. It was a comfortable experience back then. It was a seed that was planted. My brother was always called the deacon and other church relatable names. He always talked about God. As an adult, he continues to attend church every Sunday even when his wife doesn't go. Now, I truly know God. My conversations tend to always come back to him. When you realize who carried you, you inevitably live life in accordance with his word. It's mandatory.

Two weeks after the end of the world-on-fire dream, I was baptized. It was no small feat. I believe I have some type of phobia. I don't like feeling trapped. Elevators, airplanes, are fine. Being underwater and not able to breathe is not cool. One of the worst feelings is to not be able to breathe.

I wanted the relationship with God I'd heard about but, was afraid of the process I had to endure to get to it. The first experience was the baptism. I pushed through my fear because I feared going to hell more. I went back to my regular life not knowing the true meaning of what I had done. I was young. I felt relief that I was now saved. I did not know that there was a requirement to live it.

Holy Spirit

My strength comes from God. God chose me to tell my story. I don't have a choice to be anything other than great. I remembered who I am. I know that I cannot fail. When you are not afraid of failing, you can do anything. What others may see as a fail; I embrace as a win. People may think that I am weird, but I think the way the wealthy 1% think. They don't see failure, lack, or the possibility of not having enough. The secret is to believe, invest, and continue no matter what. You might fall, but you will not fail. You may be bumped and bruised, but you will not fail. The secret is bet on you. I have always gotten what I wanted. If it was within my reach, it was going to get done. If it was ever stopped, it was God. He had stopped me. Sometimes, his lessons felt like a brick to the head.

The Taxing of Ke'sha Dennis

I recognize that the Holy Spirit has been with me my entire existence. There were times when I felt alone, but I know now that the Holy Spirit was that voice in my head that told me not to do wrong or go certain places. You hear later that something bad happened, and you thank God for saving you. As a kid, it would scare me that I could see or know things before they would happen. I would tell others, and they would be shocked when it came true. I was afraid to share what I saw because I thought people would think I was crazy. I'm not psychic, but I'd have occasional premonitions. My prayer was for it to stop. I remember when we were on a bus going to my brother's wedding. There were about 60 of us. We had a game where we passed an empty bag around for everyone to add as many bills with their name written on it as they'd like. When it came around, I told my mom not to put anything in. I told my mom that my dad was going to win. My dad put two bills in, and he won over $200.

I recently went to Reno and predicted a run on the craps table. I knew the numbers that would be rolled on the dice. I get nervous and have to shut my brain down. It's a weird feeling. I feel like I'm playing with something that God doesn't want me to play with. My dreams would be so vivid they would scare me. They would come true.

I have a five-year-old right now that is called my mini-me. She is clever and mischievous. In her mind, she already knows what's going to happen. She does what she wants regardless of the circumstance.

She jumped in the car and spoke that her dad was going to cook. This man hasn't cooked in months. I got home and got to the bedroom. Her dad peeked in and asked if I wanted some of the fish and fries, he was making. That was the first time I believed she may have the gift.

At about 19, I'd practice telling myself that I will not dream, and I will not remember. I have yet to remember a dream since that time. I'm now attempting to start remembering my dreams again. I know that God will take your gifts away if you don't use them. I tell people to embrace the gifts God gave them, no matter how weird they seem. God gives each one of his children special gifts. I'm thankful for having the ability to recognize mine.

The complexity of the Mission

I am complex. I am a Rubik's cube, a never-ending puzzle. Not too many people know how to solve the Rubik's cube. When one side moves, three other sides, top and bottom move. The challenge is to orient yourself and manage the changes that are occurring on all sides. You must comprehend the puzzle as well as the process.

My anchor is God. He holds everything together. Sometimes, I can't figure myself out. He communicates with me by stopping me. Tire blow out, sickness, pulled muscles, something someone says, something I see on television. When God wants to slow me down, inevitably, I'd better pay attention to the signs.

I am reading a book about personality recognition. I am considered a thinker. The thinker must always solve something, no matter the amount of time needed to complete the task. Most people will give up, but I will go crazy until I get it. Therefore, God slows me down and occasionally stops me. He knows I will never stop.

For me, the primary drive is happiness. When it is more people working together, you become a force. You become a movement. You reach a point where you can change things. An example is my relationship with a woman who worked at Kaiser. I spoke with her early in our friendship and shared that I had always been drawn to her, by her energy. We now share scriptures. She has been on me to recognize my gifts and embrace the platform that God has gifted me with. I realized that I have a light.

We are always present in God together. I gravitate to the light in others. We are sisters and brothers of divine light. Each of us who are spiritual have this light. The light attracts other lights. The movement we create as we connect to another like soul is powerful.

I feel like a life without God is like struggling to breathe. Too many of us are trapped, unable to breathe because we are ignorant of

The Taxing of Ke'sha Dennis

the puzzle, the process, or both. I like to know there's a way out. I require deep thought when it comes to situations that can cost me my breath. Maybe it's because I've had a few scary asthma attacks. Looking around for your pump, while struggling to breathe is a terrifying experience. As a child, I was hospitalized for bronchial asthma. Any situation after that where I was threatened without breath was horrible for me.

We should be calculated in all we do. Think thoroughly before making any major decisions. Try every potential eventuality. Notice the exits. Create an escape plan. If I see no escape, the situation won't benefit me or other people. My focus must be accurate, and the energy around me must be peaceful, for me to reach my highest potential.

Draining relationships can be another struggle to breathe situation. I will cut out in a moment if the relationship isn't beneficial. Everyone is surprised when I go into Houdini mode. I don't get to that point until I have exhausted all options. I don't allow myself to be used and abused. I am aware that you think you are getting away with something. I am aware that you are taking without giving. I play dumb, but that's my character. I'm not that way in real life. I tell them people before them attempt to take advantage, yet people will always reveal their true intentions. They don't get it. I gave so many chances back then. I gave several chances to the undeserving; hoping they'd realize their faults. Now, when I see a lack of effort the first time, I look for my exit.

Everything is a puzzle and a process. Everything needs to be put together in some form. Even down to fixing a meal, there must be a plan, structure, steps, and a goal. When you have a puzzle, you see all the pieces. You don't know how they fit. You must start by connecting one to another. You can't grab 10 and connect them. You must connect two by grabbing one piece at a time.

I'm on a mission to be of service for the rest of my life. I consider it my reasonable service. Being saved now is beyond baptism. It is even beyond living a holy life. It is giving my life in service, shining my light, and drawing people to freedom. It is reasonable because my life was never mine, to begin with. God is all there is, and without him, I'm absolutely nothing.

I am like Harriet. That first slave she helped to cross over didn't make her known. How many did it take for her to get into the history books? She helped one, then another. She went back and helped more. She kept moving, motivated by the good she was doing.

I work the same way. I inspire one would-be entrepreneur to start their business. They start making money, and I go grab another entrepreneur. I continue to reach out and support others. Next thing you know, I'll have 200 launched and profitable businesses as a result of my inspiration and outreach.

Section II: Self Love

Ke'sha Dennis

Chapter 4: Rude Awakening

I was living life the right way. I was a mother, a wife, a loving caretaker, and a student. I worked so that others could be taken care of making sure to keep something going for myself. Everything that I had worked for was lost in a matter of weeks. I felt lost and uncertain for the first time in my life. Prior to this, even when my decisions had not worked out the way I planned, I was decisive. I was certain about a positive outcome. This time, I wasn't sure.

My mom was in school while I was growing up. I thought that books were fun to read. Time on punishment was spent completing book reports and writing. I would read my mother's nursing books with interest when I was eleven years old. I was determined to learn more as I got older. My great-grandmother required assistance as she got older. I was a great help to her. This furthered my sense of fit for helping as a profession. I wanted to be a registered nurse.

I stayed in nursing school through 3 pregnancies. I was going to be a RN no matter what. My other two children came after nursing school. School was never a chore for me. The success I experienced with puzzles and math in my earlier educational experiences was a comfort for me as I progressed. School was a means to an end. It was also a way to satisfy my curiosity. I wanted as much information as possible.

I am a sponge. If it is something new, I want to know everything about it. I will break it down to the molecular level and absorb it. I want to know the origin, why it was created, who was involved. I live my

The Taxing of Ke'sha Dennis

life like Dora the Explorer. Every day is an adventure for me. I'm excited about the clues God leaves me to find the treasures in life. That's what happens when you are born and raised in Berkeley, CA.

I continued to go to school because I knew I'd make more than the minimum wage. I naively thought I could keep going to school until I made it to CEO. I didn't know the career ladder or the chain of command. They didn't teach us that in school. All I saw was a registered nurse and the money she made. My great grandmother needed help. I helped her. So, I knew I had something to offer in the helping field. My mother was a nurse helping people, so I figured I'd do that. The farther I advanced in the nursing program, the more I realized about my future profession. I didn't like much about the nursing besides talking to the patients. That was my favorite part. But I was not going to quit.

That One Old Lady Teacher

I always wondered why this teacher was still teaching. She was well into her 70s. Had to be. It was a semester I have never forgotten and an experience that shaped me and my career. We were instructed to study a set of information from a study guide. When we got the test, the questions were different from everything the teacher told us to study. The students gathered together after the test to compare notes. It was clear to us that there must have been some sort of mistake. We decided as a group to go to the teacher and air our concerns. We arrived to talk, and the only person talking was Ke'sha. I was comfortable speaking. I considered that I was simply providing a voice to what the other students were hesitant to say. I thought adult dialogue was warranted and to be celebrated.

The day after our conversation, the teacher had an attitude. From there, I knew she had it in for me. She failed me in clinicals because she couldn't fail me in the classroom assignments. I made all A's and B's until the disagreement about the test. Her accusation for clinicals was that I left the room before my patient swallowed her pills. It was a

Ke'sha Dennis

trumped-up charge with no basis in fact. But it was an offence that could result in failure. She pursued it to show me who was boss.

She showed me who was boss. I didn't know that a teacher could do what she did. I thought that people in those positions were obligated to tell the truth. Prior to this unfortunate reality, I was living in Care Bear land. I didn't know about institutional racism. I used to go to my white neighbor's house and eat guava and play with her dog. I didn't realize that a teacher could hold a grudge. I was always a favorite student.

I brought these shattered misconceptions home. My children's father explained that these behaviors extended to teachers, nurses, and even policemen. He taught me a lot about the police. Police were frequent visitors to the neighborhood he came from. I thought police officers were sworn in to tell the truth. I thought they were focused on protecting and serving. I swore in as a nurse, and I obligated myself never to leave others without care. I committed to doing no harm. I thought that spirit lived in others. It is not that I have not done anything wrong or have never lied, but I repent and make it a point to stay away from repeating poor behavior. To see someone lie with a straight face after doing someone wrong perplexed me.

After she failed me, I knew the policy. A student must fail twice to be dismissed from the program. I was shaken but not deterred. She told her fellow research teacher to fail me too. I was seeing the cruelty in the world. I was seeing how ugly people could be. It became real to me. I don't understand how people can live doing wrong, and it does not occur to them that change is needed.

The assignment was patient to nurse ratio paper worth 20 points. I proposed that nurses should have less than five patients. I utilized qualitative and quantitative measures to support my thesis. I showed my paper to another nursing research teacher. She scored me 18 out of 20. Other students commented that my paper was better than 80 percent of papers from the class. I know that I did an excellent job on that paper. I needed 11 points to pass. That lady gave me a 6.

The school was a private institution. I now know that this makes a difference in how teachers like this can hide and survive while doing their dirt. This teacher had done this to 3 different students that I know of. It was a rude awakening in my life, but I didn't awaken right away. I know it was a conspiracy because when I went to the board review, it took 5 of those women to stand against me to plead their case. Five teachers came and sat against me. What an honor that was. I saw how powerful God made me in that moment.

How Dare God!

It was 2008. I was devastated. My life consisted of waking, caring for home, school, and repeat. After that experience, I lost that sense of living life the right way. I considered that I was a great student in comparison to other students. I agonized about who I could have been. My devastation quickly turned to anger. "How dare God!"

I felt that the teacher was intimidated. I knew so much from my experience with my mother. I had been in the hospital and care of my husband with sickle cell. I would ask so many questions. It is a recurring theme in my life. People get in their feelings in my personal relationship due to their inadequacies or lack of ability to communicate effectively. For my part, I want everyone to win. If only they wanted to win as much as I do and realized, we can both win. They wait for the pie to get made. Then, they want a slice. I will take you to the water, but once there, you must drink.

I felt like everything had been taken away from me. I had worked my whole life to get this degree. I felt lost. I didn't know what I was going to do. I didn't have another plan. I have never been a plan B type of person. What the hell do you do when plan A is snatched away from you. To have someone take it away from me, hold on. It felt like quicksand. I couldn't understand how something that I knew to be wrong could go through. It was a hard truth about being an African

Ke'sha Dennis

American woman in America. At some point, we are all going to get that lesson. I don't care how high up you get or how smart you are.

I was Kesha Dennis, who always got what she wanted. What do you mean Kesha can't get a nursing degree? I could get anything I wanted. I understood after that experience that God alone has been the one stopping me to bless me with more. It took a good 4 to 5 years to understand that this experience was a blessing.

Chapter 5: Wilding Out

I started hanging out. "I'm going to start living like everyone else, free." I was like, "Forget everything!" Forget life. God failed me. I was going to fail him. Someone should've told me that you can't pay God back. I cursed God for allowing me to be kicked out of nursing school. I cursed God for what I now know he saved me from. I had a dream that was not completely my own. I maintained a vision that was the product of my youth without the benefit of knowing myself. But I directed my disappointment and rage at the situation toward God. I didn't want to be the good girl anymore. Since that didn't work, I was determined to try something different.

When you are filled with Yeshua's spirit, you must replace that with other spirits (alcohol) that'll allow you to rebel. I started hanging out partying and drinking socially. I previously believed that hanging out wasn't what a mother of three should do. I was always the caretaker, ever the responsible one. I decided to be irresponsible; it's not like I had a class to go to.

That period of my life lasted four years. I felt like I was doing the same thing every single day, but there was never a day I felt accomplished. That lack of accomplishment, the lack of progress, eventually led to a change. As soon as the hanging out and social drinking ended, I recognized that His spirit was present with me. I was always safe, protected, and guided. In my rebellion, I found myself in situations where terrible things could have happened, but He protected me.

Through it all, he never left me. That's how great he is. Even though I'm undeserving, he still loved me. There is no greater love. He has always been in me. I have always felt him.

The different glimpses of my childhood; seeing people grow up on my block, right across the street from the park. It changed drastically. I had to take care of other kids before I was out of my childhood myself. I didn't feel the decline of the neighborhood like others because, of the functionality of my home. There were kids on my block I'd cook for. I knew they weren't eating many good home-cooked meals, so I figured it was my job to make sure they ate. We had lots of food, so why not share?

It took me a little bit of partying to determine that that life wasn't for me. I didn't feel productive. I missed learning new things and meeting new people. My determination began coming back. I had the desire to feed my brain again. My desire to help others was reborn.

The First Awakening

I was an old maid at 16. No one should be a live-in nurse and a homebound mother that young. I felt like (2003) I met Herb and began hanging out with him. We developed a friendship. He was a basketball player. I was 310 pounds then. I gained 140 pounds between my first and second child. I didn't know I was that big. I thought I was 170 pounds in my mind. He was fun and adventurous. He could do all the things that my husband could not. I was super attracted. I had the comfort of my husband paying all the bills. A relationship with Herb would be a major change from what I was used to.

I was more intentional, but my target was wrong. I found myself projecting into another relationship what I should've been injecting into myself. It began to drain my soul. I had to stop investing unconditionally into others and begin putting that same energy into me. I didn't realize how broken I was. But I was willing to do my work.

We can all get there. We just must do the work. We sometimes dig deep to make up a whole story and believe it. Until you can let that

The Taxing of Ke'sha Dennis

go, continue to do your work. Be quiet. Be still. Watch. Confirm it with God. Go to the holy spirit for confirmation and clarity. I was only confused because I allowed confusion into my life. I can see the king in a man that others may overlook. My African studies teacher in high school taught me about Black male and female relationships. Although many men are broken, their lives a king within many of them.

You could not tell me ten years ago that I didn't love myself. I wasn't aware that I was 310 pounds. I didn't know I was broken. I vowed never to feel incomplete again. I knew I had serious work to do. I started recognizing that my weight was a problem. Woman need to stop taking care of everyone else and turn that focus on ourselves. I know that I should have been investing in myself. I began climbing up the stairs towards a different life one at a time. I was breathing overtime. I felt like my heart was beating out of my chest. I started looking at myself in the mirror. I didn't recognize myself. My head was down, and I looked up seven years later, 125lbs overweight. I was taking care of my kids. I was attending school. I was taking care of my husband. I know it sounds insane. But I didn't know. Then, when you recognize it, the guilt and shame is overwhelming.

My aunt was in a food anonymous group. She invited me to one of their meetings. I could not fully relate. I didn't feel like my eating was out of control. But I did feel that my diet needed to drastically change. I was eating the wrong things at the wrong time. It's a free program. I would advise people who are overweight to take advantage of it. It will educate you on your needs. It jumpstarted my weight loss.

It took me ten months to lose 125 pounds. I would go to the gym four days a week for ten months and get trained by coach Compton and Waduda. During this time, my husband was sick a lot. I spent my time taking care of him. I never took time for me. I was 172lbs when I met him. By the time I had my second daughter, my weight was spiraling out of control. I was 125 pounds overweight. "How did I allow myself to become 310lbs?" was a constant thought? My heart dropped. I had two daughters and couldn't make it upstairs. I was afraid I'd have a heart attack if I didn't do something about it. I was attending Merritt College in Oakland, CA. I walked into the gym without thinking and immediately got active.

Done with Responsibility but Reality Check

In 2009, I ran back into Herb. I had been running around hanging out for a year when I ran into him again. I busted out at 25 years old and started hanging out a lot. I felt like I was released from prison. I never did any hard drugs. I grew up in the 1990s when beautiful families were torn apart by drugs, so I knew to stay away from them. I saw how people could just change seemingly overnight. We were together almost every day and every night. It was 2011 when I got pregnant by Herb, and things got real.

The baby brought everything to the light. I did many ugly things I am not proud of during that time. It is embarrassing and degrading when you are so hurt that you want everyone involved to be hurt too. It was not cool, and I have grown tremendously from those past hurts. I have recently come to the revelation it was ungodly and outside Yeshua's favor. Although it's hard to forget the hurt, it would be ungodly not to do God's will because of past shame. Moving forward, after repentance, in a healthy direction is a choice to embrace without shame.

Chapter 6: God Politics

Cursing God

I was out of school and didn't know what I was going to do. I started cursing God. School was good to me with grants and loans. I was making it on the strength of that money. I was 30 about this time, and I was nine years behind my 21-year-old allowance to drinking. I always felt like the life I was leading was the life I was supposed to lead.

I had never experienced something that I worked for being taken away. What I really wanted to do is curse out all the teachers at the school. I knew that this would not make me feel better, so I acted out like a kid would do. I don't think people in positions of authority understand the impact they have on people's lives and livelihood. They were not just denying a grade. Especially when they victimize and lie, trauma is perpetrated on an overwhelming scale. Feeling a dream stripped away is simply not cool. I made the decision to say, "Forget it!"

I was blocking God out. I refused my mother's invitations to Bible study. I was not giving God the time He deserves. We know when we are being disobedient. I didn't feel any sensations while in that space. My mental strength allowed me to erase the experience and rewrite it to my preference. I just need to be done with a situation, and I'm moving on with life as if it never happened.

I didn't know this was a gift. Now, I pray for her. If I could talk to that teacher now, I would tell her thank you. No matter how bad someone has done me, I pray for their soul. I pray for their soul because I know God's wrath is coming. I serve God, and I know that he takes care of his own. So, I pray. I must. I would hate to be a hurt soul again. I would hate to be that ugly, mean, vindictive, and broken again. It must be hard to consistently live that way. Living that life, you are going to be miserable. I appreciate elders and children for their resilience.

I didn't think that he could forgive me. I know that God forgives, but I'd cursed him. I don't get how after we realize his love, we don't try our best to be more like him. You don't have a choice after you treat God like that. It is a testament to his eternal patience and longsuffering that my family was still safe and taken care of after my disrespect. I felt completely unworthy. Now that I know the peace, he desired for me; I wouldn't want it any other way. I don't know how I was living before.

My Rebellion

I was a Stepford wife who remained in school. What I was finding in my rebellion was a taste of the freedom that I thought was selfish, but I did not fully understand. On the other hand, I started to see that people were having a more fun life than me. Understand, I was a nurse-maid for almost a decade. Being constantly disrespected by my ex-husband's mom. I believed that there was something more out there; I knew there was something better. I wanted something better, but I had not visualized my future yet.

I am spontaneous and a quick mover. The thought of "why not" motivates me. I have an idea of what I want to do, and I am going to do it. The adventure during my nurse-maid years was the world of education and books. I was touching cadavers, picking through literal brains, learning molecules, and studying biology. I had several fun moments throughout this time. I created my own pockets of happiness in those moments. I may not have been absent physically, but mentally, I'm out; if not mentally stimulated. The switch to getting out physically revealed how exhausted I was. It took me a while to transition, but I had to find something to occupy my mind.

Later, I would understand that it was not God I was upset with. I was a kid having a temper tantrum. He always let me get my way. Determination defines me. The lesson was needed because I needed to learn to listen. It wasn't other people saying no. It was Him saying, "Sometimes, you must be still and listen." It had been difficult in the past, but now I get it. It took some hard falls, but I get it. The thing about determined people is that they need to know when to stop and let go. It is our biggest flaw.

The Second Awakening

Every ten years, I seem to experience a significant awakening in my life. You will have shifts as well when you determine to improve your situation. It is like a chicken emerging out of the shell or a butterfly emerging from a chrysalis. The protections of infancy and nurturing fall away as you seek to mature. It's more of a come through than a breakthrough. Your job is to endure as you learn.

I was misinformed about Yeshua. I realized that I am not here for what society says I should be. I'm here for what God called me to be. Doing nothing, being nothing and hanging out gave me perspective. I was not going anywhere. Everyone around me was either not bright or hadn't tapped into their light. I felt it in my spirit. I was disgusted with the place I found myself in. I knew God called me to be greater than that. I didn't feel like my life was mine anymore. I was not progressing in the ways that I wanted. Something was missing. I didn't feel like I had completed my puzzle. I could not do the same thing every day and expect different results. I had to think about that and shift.

When others shift, they will be gung-ho in the first day or first month, and they will eventually give up. Maybe the results are not happening fast enough, or maybe they're not learning what they want. You must reprogram your brain to expect varying degrees of progress.

Ke'sha Dennis

Some days you may have less productive days, some days there's no progress at all. You can't give up, no matter what. It is not in you to give up. When you feel that you are about giving up, pray. God will take over. You must move. Don't worry about all the need; he'll take care of everything. Do the next best thing you can think of and add to your pot each day until you see progress.

God is freedom. In my brain, I believed that I had to rebel, and through a temper tantrum. I later realized I wasn't doing anything outside the norm. How could I say that I was a child of God if I did things he disapproved of? I wanted to stay within the realm of controlling myself. God teaches his controlling kids the art of letting go. I appreciated that lesson. I knew growth would come from these experiences. Finding that freedom in Yeshua is knowing that I was right the whole time. Everything I wanted was and is obtainable through Him. I just had to gain the clarity of vision, see my uniqueness, and ask for help. That's the come through.

I decided to regroup and go back to school. I realized who I was. I'm a lifetime learner. I enrolled in the University of Phoenix to provide me with the flexibility I needed. I enrolled in a degree option that better fit MY aspirations, personality, and interests. It cost me another $40,000, but what I took away was priceless. Once I received my degree, I was back.

School was not about receiving the training that experience would teach, but it was a gathering of like-minded people who were committed to improving themselves. It was a collection of teachers who understood the challenges of the adult learner. Both provided space for me to come into my own. I now know that the world is open to me. Travel, investment, self-knowledge. When you don't have that opportunity presented young, you are at a disadvantage. It wasn't the direction that I would have chosen, but looking at me know, I needed all that to become the person that I am today.

The Taxing of Ke'sha Dennis

I can't just sit. I must see the next picture. Everyone tells me to slow down. People are telling me that I move too fast. In my mind, I'm saying, "Catch up." If you hear it long enough, you must reflect and grow. I need people around me that are vocal and real. I must find a balance because the whole world doesn't tell the same lie. My Chief Financial Officer Aisha is one of those people. I believe God sends you those angels in life exactly when you need them.

Every aspect of life has politics. No one can have control over my life. I used to care what people thought. That must have been the source of the discomfort with sharing or fear. I now know who I am and what I want because of my life experiences. I am ready to fly. I am getting rid of the weights that were holding me back. The secret is to know who you are. Claim your "I am" again.

Chapter 7: The Return

Lessons Learned

You need to know that God is never going to leave you. Looking back, I realized that God was there the whole time. Today, I feel like it was delusion and craziness. Anyone who would curse God like I did would have to be crazy. I am sure that God would say, "There's another one of my disobedient children. I keep giving her chances, and she's not getting the message." It had to be a conversation about me. There must have been a greater plan for me to get the lesson right around age 40. My objective with the rebellion was to disassociate myself from the thought of my spiritual connection. When you are in the middle of the storm, you just feel like it is effed up. If God allows the effed up, maybe I was effed up too. But it wasn't in me. Here I am trying to hang with these people, and it just wasn't me. It wasn't going to work.

Never allow someone the power to control your destiny. In nursing school, I was in a position where someone could take what I had worked for. She made up a lie and connected with another teacher to blackball me. She knew that my failing out of one program would make it difficult to be in another. It was a calculated frame-up. Now, I am in control of my own destiny. I don't allow people to come between me and my money or my time. I march to the beat of God's drum. He has given me leeway to control my position. He allowed me to be in a position of ownership. I don't see myself going backward. As long as I can continue learning, I don't have a vulnerability to the lives of others.

Just because you get out of behavior, doesn't me you get out of who you are. I thought I could act like a different person and become her. But you are who you are. I had a forget it attitude when it came to responsibility, during that period in my life. I had been responsible so long, for my siblings, my mother, my husband, my children. I didn't want to take care of anyone anymore. I was drained.

I am adventurous. I am inquisitive. I am all about the puzzle. Once I get done with the puzzle, I find another one to start. Like Forrest Gump running. He was running and growing a huge beard. When he stopped, he was done. That's me.

I just discovered my mantra while writing. When I am engaged with activities, I consider a puzzle-solving approach, as a method of figuring things out. What's missing? What do I need to add? What do I need to subtract? What do I need to do to make this work for me? As in the Matrix trilogy, the oracle was the orchestrator through the whole movie. She always gave you clues to figure out the answer.

New School

Often, my mind is jumbled with ideas and thoughts. This time was a period of clear thought. It was like having a regular S1 diamond compared to a flawless diamond. One is cloudy, including flaws. The other is clear. It was a perfect thought. "This is what you do. You do it well." I was too old to be doing what others were doing. People told me that I was missing something. I never thought I was missing anything. Why was I listening to them anyway? If you have four broke friends and you hang around them every day, you will be the fifth. I've learned from these experiences to stop listening to others and follow my own heart no matter what.

Ke'sha Dennis

I remember thinking about how I could utilize my nursing school credits and not waste them. I don't know how the University of Phoenix became an option, but I'm glad it was. I could attend one day per week. The rest was online. The learning environment was exciting for me. A huge whiteboard, stimulating conversation, and a well-lit space is my high. Give me that over any drug. Being in a learning atmosphere with people who want to learn and do more is exciting for me.

I had many bomb teachers while in Phoenix. One made the materials relatable. He allowed us into his personal life. He would sit back and allow us to teach him. A student can learn from a teacher, and a teacher can learn from students as well. I wish the world would get rid of titles because we all learn from one another. People think they are their title. Just because someone has the title, they shouldn't automatically receive respect. Respect must be earned through your actions. People sometimes feel that titles allow them to be superior. But last time I checked; God made us all equal. I go by the Bible, the first shall be last, and the last shall be first. People like that are not going anywhere.

I also met some cool lifelong friends at Phoenix. One, Jolene. She almost shares birthday with me. She is one of those people that keeps it almost too real. She still makes time for me, even with the responsibilities of her personal life. I love having strong women around me. It feeds my spirit!

I attended University of Phoenix and completed my degree. Bachelor of Science in Health Administration and Management. I chose that because it was still in the health field. I was determined to gain the degree I worked for. As I thought more about it, management was my cup of tea. I am comfortable leading a team. It was perfect.

I began working at a biotech corporation as a case manager on the rheumatoid arthritis team. It was a contract job making about $40 per hour. I never intended on having my own business, but I knew I'd format it somewhat like theirs. I next worked as a senior consultant in a hospital. It was a cutthroat atmosphere. It felt like I was in the 13th grade of high school surrounded by a bunch of selfish, cutthroat people.

The Financial Trap

I soon enrolled in the MBA/MHA program at University of Phoenix but never completed. I realized that school was a scam. Or, I realized the value of the educational system. At its core, it is not about degrees or learning. It is about relationships and networks. If you don't take away that value, you are not getting your money's worth.

There are not a lot of people that speak my language. I am working to update my circle of friends. I need people that are on my level. I am a bit of a nerd. I wouldn't mind a trip to Barnes & Noble. I like to go to Bed Bath & Beyond and see what new technological advances they've reached in household items. I love checking out their new hypothermic pillows. I know it sounds corny to some, but I'm different, and I love it. I want to find out what's new. What is Elon Musk doing? How did he get the permit to build those tunnels underground without the knowledge of what he was going to do? Let me go sit in the room with him. I'd have the time of my life picking his brain for information.

I was going to school to get a job, I thought. As I have said, I thought I would go to school, graduate, and be the CEO. I thought I was worth a quarter million right out of school. I was expecting a salary of at least $200,000. I was living a fairy tale and was awakened to a world where people don't care about anyone and good luck if you ever make it to manager, let alone CEO.

Are we all just going to stand and pretend that the emperor has clothes? The world is changing to a social program that is devoid of a prosocial reality. Yet, it is under the disguise of being prosocial. No one's world is in interaction. Everyone is in their phone.

Chapter 8: Breakout from Norms

Rebellion can be positive. When you are in the pits of despair, your fight or flight motivates the search for a way out. Your survival instinct kicks in full force. We often think of rebellion as running away from something, usually responsibility. My experience was being disillusioned with the truth I had been taught. I attempted to live the opposite of it. And I couldn't. It wasn't because the truth of me was a lie. It was because the truth of how I should navigate the world was a lie. I didn't have to live according to their rules and standards.

You feel it when you find yourself. The holy spirit talks to you silently. It moves through you. You realize that what you are into is not it. Being true to who you are, you can't run away from that. It doesn't matter how fast or hard you run. God will make his children come back. Once the seed is planted, it will grow.

Most people want God to tell them what they want to hear. They can be praying for a revelation, but it comes as the truth. It doesn't come as comfort and ease. It comes as the ability to walk through the pain, fear of embarrassment, fear of rejection, the valley of the shadow of death and win. We are fixated on a success that is superficial. But lasting truth comes like gems. They are rare but precious and valuable.

Moving from Jesus to Yeshua: Enlightenment

The connection is the name for what we have lost. We don't have the fortitude to walk through the pain because we don't feel we have the back up or support from the people that matter most. Experience in church and religious settings demonstrates this well. People are caught up in the wording and reverence of the religious texts and religious practices rather than the spiritual realities and spiritual practices. People can do the thing that makes them a member but fail to honor, seek justice, or demonstrate compassion. I may not remember the name and scripture, but I remember the feeling I have when truly connecting with a passage of scripture.

People feel that they are closer to Jesus. They get indignant and self-righteous proclaiming, "I go to church, and you don't!"

My reaction is simple and straightforward: "You're throwing money and time away. I'm not!"

We are visual and we respond in some way to logic, wisdom, and information. Read for yourself. Research. Read about how every culture has a version of the birth of a savior story. Search out how Christianity doesn't fit a consistent pattern of history, culture, and ethnicity. The answers are out there. What you will find are questions that may pull you away from the words and the religion toward the feeling and the spirit. You will recognize the need for a shift in mindset toward connection. You will begin to ask about ways to more intimately and holistically connect in service and justice.

When you choose not to get your own answers. That's a choice of ignorance. That choice of ignorance makes you a fool. And I can no longer align myself with fools. I feel it's my duty to reveal truths and facts. We all should be looking for answers. Or, we could stay on Instagram and Facebook and look pretty (Sarcastic!).

Mindset

The pressure is on for women to look good and fit societies standards. When you submit to that mindset, you are always in a position of throwing unnecessary money away, to fit in. That's why the beauty industry is a multi-billion-dollar industry. Be smart and invest in stocks with the money you'd normally spend on hair, nails, clothes and shoes. We must stop throwing our money down the drain.

I have spent money on a tummy tuck. You give in to the pressures of staying in shape and looking right. It is social programming. You see the models and templates on television. I'm not against spending money to on feeling good in your skin, but we should limit our spending.

Yet, no one desires to be fat. Anyone who tells you they desire it is lying. I was the fattest chick in the room at one point at over 300 pounds. No one can tell me that it feels good. It doesn't. That's health. Get support if you don't know how to address your weight issues. Health is wealth, and you can't spend your money if you're not alive.

Where I come from, getting support or any form of therapy was a bad thing. Whether it was drug addiction, deficiency, or disease, help was a problem. The narrative is changing now. Getting therapy is considered a good thing. You need that professional support. People who are not in your situation don't understand. It takes professional insight or a support group of people who are or have been where you are. So many support groups exist for whatever you are going through or want to know.

I have never really cared about what people said outside my family. I see a lot of people who go through that. I had to gain an understanding of how people could not change their mindset and do something different. I had to walk into a support group and see what the barriers were people faced. I met so many people with similar stories that helped others. I saw people succeeding toward their goals.

If we invested as much in our internal as our external, we would have the means to be happy. I went to another country, and everyone was happier. In America, everyone is striving for the Hollywood look.

Change Coming

I see a change coming. Women are networking with women. People are looking each other in the eye and connecting. We are

The Taxing of Ke'sha Dennis

recognizing our common struggle and acknowledging that we need each other. The support I witnessed in groups I attended became a model for me.

It is less of a business plan and more like a lifestyle. I have the pieces in order in my brain. It is evolving. My CFO is teaching me how to write out my vision. I think, say, and move. I need to think, write, say, then move. That synergy is required. When I see my CFO, I am energized. Being alone in your thoughts is different from being with someone who can understand your thoughts and see your vision. Having someone who can operationalize your thoughts is priceless. That is how you get to extraordinary success.

The networking group is Lady Buzz. The group was originally created for anyone attempting to network and share business ideas. It was a barter of information group. You could sell your items and services for profit, so that everyone could make money and grow their business. The group was to initiate the contacts.

The next was to create the platform. That allowed me to connect through speaking engagements. It creates the foundation. So many people need motivation. A lot of people don't have the necessary information to change; my Facebook group Lady Buzz is the platform for the conversation that creates movement. It becomes infectious when you see entrepreneurs growing their businesses daily.

Next was the branding. People want to know who they are engaging with. I've hired a marketing team to reach the masses. There are many ways to grow your business online, but make sure to do the research before choosing what approach to take.

After that, you build your team. They are the interpreters that can understand my vision, vibe, and connect it to vehicles. That's what separates the CEOs from the workers. They are separate. They are not talking to the masses a lot of the time, because they're usually busy learning new skill sets to grow the business. They are visioning and creating. They don't have time for anything else. It's not that they are being mean. They are constantly working. They are constantly thinking and managing. If they must stop for everything, they can't make their vision come to life. Sometimes we need to unplug from society and put all that energy into ourselves.

Once that's accomplished, you work the vision. You extend the opportunity. That is success.

Section III: Spirit

Chapter 9: Taxes

The contract at Kaiser was coming to an end. I found out through some connections that I could make close to 6 figures in 3 months doing taxes. I knew what I could do with six figures. It's never been hard for me to make money. It was the thought of making it that fast. I could not believe there was a way to make it that fast with taxes. It wouldn't be until I saw the money come in that I believed her. People can say things. I take it at face value when they talk. I must see it to believe.

I decided to take a chance on me. I didn't realize at the time that this was what I was doing. Then, I felt like I did not have much to lose. Even if I make a cool amount of money, it would be better than nothing. I certainly didn't think that I could make a career out of it.

My vision is larger than that. I am interested in real estate. I want to travel, speak, and encourage people. Taxes is a good steppingstone. Steppingstones are important. I have made $10 per hour before, so I understand humility well. The whole time I worked for that amount, I knew I was worth more than that. I didn't wallow in the fact that I was in the situation. I focused on my next move. I used it as motivation to push forward. It was another puzzle that I had to figure out. So, if taxes were going to be a steppingstone, I was going to do it until I make my next move. My next move was my best move. I found that this opportunity made greater opportunities possible. That teaches me that my next move will open new opportunities.

The Taxing of Ke'sha Dennis

I was that woman who would exclaim, "Ten dollars. I can't even get gas for that!" You must eat a large slice of that humble pie. You must go into that job like it's the best job ever until you find your next move. My grandmother said, "You never know who you are going to meet. Be the best in everything you do." We stuck out like sore thumbs because we were taught to say Yes, Please, and Thank You. My mom and grandma stressed the importance of proper verbiage and etiquette.

Leap of Faith

When my contract ended, I took a leap of faith and did two months of taxes and made almost a year's worth of income. From the moment that I started working, my first check came two a week later. After that, the checks came weekly and sometimes twice a week. It was multiple thousands and added up extremely fast. It was $72,000 that first tax season.

The excitement fizzled due to unexpected circumstances. It didn't fit right in my spirit, so I worked with another person. After a while, I felt like I was working as an employee. My input didn't seem relevant. If I'm not heard, I become quiet. I was looking for the escape hatch. I didn't know how to start a business. I knew that it was cool to educate people about their finances, but I never planned on becoming a business owner. I saw that many people in need of help. I knew that I could grow my business by educating people about financial literacy.

I was back at square one. I didn't think about having my own business. God had other plans. I am not sure when I created a vision board. Sometime around 2013 or 2014. I always take pictures of my vision boards. I was going through my photos, and my red vision board pops up. The word God was written in sharpie on the top, bottom, and both sides. I wanted to make sure that God protected everything on board. Success. Win it All. Jumpstart your weight loss. Flat abs now. I homed into one little box that read, "Start your own business."

Ke'sha Dennis

Breaking Chains

I had a four-year-old, seven-year-old, thirteen-year-old, and a nineteen-year-old that were depending on me. I didn't think I could do it and it wasn't easy. I had to get everyone to chip in where they could. I bought my daughter a car so she could help get the kids to school. Of course, no one can do it like mom. But you can't be in every place at one time. Sometimes their hair is not going to look right. Sometimes they will have mismatched socks. I had to get detached from society's pressure for moms to handle everything perfectly.

You are not a bad mom or a bad person if it takes you a couple of days to get to their hair. We must break free of those chains. The richest mom drives the beat-up car and had the child who dresses himself. She is a boss with multiple things on her plate.

I love when women like Oprah reveal themselves. They strip away their makeup and show themselves to be real women. They encourage women to stop trying to be the women they see in magazines. I used to be that woman who spent the gang of money to get her hair done all the time. I liked different hairstyles. I am now comfortable with a ponytail and a hat. I had to break free.

To see what two years will do is crazy. I sit around and look at the walls in my office. To be in a place where you can do what you want when you want is a feeling of freedom.

There have been struggles. There are times when I cry. I wouldn't want it any other way. I can spend time with my kids when I want to. I can spend time with myself when I want to. There is nothing like a sense of freedom. I remember feeling that if I go to the bathroom too many times, someone can say something. I remember thinking, "That shouldn't even be a thought for a grown woman. I shouldn't have to feel like I'm being watched all the time." It was being under surveillance. I had to break free.

I tell my children to learn to navigate through life like the game of life. I tell them you can go the family route and struggle, or you can go

The Taxing of Ke'sha Dennis

to college, take some time to figure out responsibility, and create a solid foundation. I focus on the associate degree in business and classes in accounting. I don't believe there's a need for a 4-year college. I want them prepared to fill the spaces where I am weak. I want them to start a business before they get out of college. That reality provides them with a means to go anywhere and hit the ground running.

"Stay with me long enough and I will brainwash you to believe that you are great." People tell me that I inspire them. What I do is ask them about their favorite thing to do. Some may say they like to build. Others say they like to braid. I am immediately in business mode. I tell them what they can do and the steps they need to take. They all say, "I never thought of it like that." The seed is planted, and they will come back. They will begin to see it as attainable because it is attainable.

I remember one chastisement experience with my 20-year-old. She's a go-getter. She lands the job. The first day, she was late. When I talked to her, she responded, "It was just training." For me, it is a time management issue—a foundational issue. That was an eye-opener for me. She showed me myself and my need to model greater time management skills. The urgency is not the same for my kids as it was for me growing up. It is up to me to support a sense of responsibility even while the dire urgency does not exist.

I think my daughter is like me, or like I was. She doesn't see herself sometimes, or she isn't aware of her capabilities in the context of her opportunities. I had to find that awareness on my own. She has me, so she doesn't have to wait until she finds it on her own. Sometimes, it takes a person around you to tell you who you appear to be. If you don't like it, you change it. If you don't change, that's who you are. Period. You will have haters. We don't care what they think. But the people we consider as our supporters, confidants, or those we are called to serve can speak life into us in ways that we don't realize.

And we intend to communicate value to them as well. If they are not feeling and engaging based on value, you must reevaluate what you are providing. The goal is to communicate with the same energy and look for that energy to be returned in kind. I have learned to live this way. I'm teaching my daughter to do the same.

Chapter 10: Being Shaped

My 40th birthday trip was planned for the Dominican Republic. I knew I needed to think and grow. I told my sister-friend, Victoria that if she didn't come with me to the Dominican Republic, I was going to die. I said it because I knew there was something better in life for me. I felt trapped and did not feel complete. I needed this trip out of the country, to have a spiritual awakening.

I planned to go with my children's father. But God had other plans. I needed to take this trip alone, with no immediate family. I cried, I danced, I journaled. I used the solitude for growth. I was able to do things I never thought about doing. I jumped from a cave. I drank a Dominican tea. My sister from another mother, Victoria, doesn't understand how much that meant to me. It's important to surround yourself with people that want to see you happy.

I stepped into the ocean and spoke to God, "I am leaving everything that is a problem in the United States, in this Dominican water."

That was the second awakening. The food was better. There was no racism. I had not felt that good in a long time. Upon my return, I was ready. I was ready to start my business and take on the world.

Not Paying Dues But Being Shaped

I had not paid all my dues, but it wasn't dues he was concerned about. I realized that I was being shaped. I had not brought all the pieces and life lessons together. In life, certain things happen that get you ready for other events. God knows his children. He knew that I had to be put in a position to listen.

Now, I sit still and take the time to listen. I can only hear when it is quiet. It is never quiet if it is up to me. I must be intentional about going to a quiet space. When you are busy, you think about too much and overload yourself. Just like those in the Bible would go into gardens and mountain retreats to pray, I must now isolate myself to hear the message of the Holy Spirit.

Women have an extra burden in comparison to men. We have a secret language that allows us to communicate together. We know that we will have to juggle a sick child and more. We should not see it as dues. We should see where God is leading and teaching us in every situation. I have learned to listen to that leading. Every time I would do things myself, it doesn't end like I would have liked.

There are differences and similarities between men and women. Men have a bro code and a language as well. It may not go as deep as people try to make it. The two sexes understand things on different levels. We can come together and create something useful. Women can come together and create something special. The females in most species are revered. It seems that women in the human species are degraded or diminished. That diminishing limits the positive impact of women to influence the greatness of a man. An ambitious, curious, intellectual, and learning woman can build a man into a great man. And these are only a few of the adjectives that we can use. There doesn't have to be a finite expression or a closed-ended view of the potential and the power of women.

Communication is key. Ask questions. Listen. See where you belong. Find your position. Stand strong in your position. Find your gift. Develop it. Make it powerful and share it. Then, bottle it and brand it. As a tax preparer, I won't hang out with people talking about opening an assisted living facility. If you are upping your skillset, engage with people that are exchanging the information that grows your brand.

The Taxing of Ke'sha Dennis

People look at the money that comes from an activity, and they go after that. But they are attracted by the benefits. They don't know or want to engage in the work it takes. You have friends and family that feel that they should be making the money you are making. They don't, and they become envious as a result. They need to be supported into their own business. Getting into other people's business will set you up for failure. You must focus on your brand. If you are not making the moves they are making or doing the numbers they are doing, you will be disappointed. You will put that disappointment in the atmosphere, and you attract greed, envy, and jealousy. You are only getting that because you are in someone else's business.

Ugly Process

I began to make a good amount of money. I shared it. The people that I shared my accomplishments with became envious. They started saying and acting ways that I had not seen before. My attempts to share and inspire had the opposite effect. Sometimes, people twist what you are trying to say into their own thoughts. When someone reveals themselves, you must treat them with a long handled spoon.

Once you separate, you are faced with you in the mirror. It is like going into a cocoon. When you go into that space, you are taking the time to butterfly yourself. You are developing into who you were meant to be. You were never meant to be a caterpillar. Caterpillars don't know that they are to become butterflies. Caterpillars begin to create their chrysalis, believing they are creating their tombs. They think that they are going to die.

It is only in God's time that you build that chrysalis and pull into that cocoon. It is not isolation. You can hear the world around you. You are not completely unattached. It is not about a cold, dark room by yourself. It is not a time of depression and mistrust of yourself. These are moments of solitude to think clearly and listen carefully. Go to the water or the spa or whatever separates you from the normal hustle and bustle. When you get into that space, you will grow.

Those moments are filled with affirmations, prayer, meditation, understanding, evaluation, growth, understanding, serenity, praise, worship, love, and compassion for self. Your time is not a cycle of low thinking and despair. It is a time of renewal. We can get ugly when we're alone in prayer. You may have tears. Snot may be running. Slob may drool. But at that point, you are your most open to God. You may not understand how you pull through certain situations. God carries you in those moments. We have all felt alone until we realize who has carried us. Just like the caterpillar, you may not know what the next stage is. But continue to meditate until you emerge. You will see your wings and know that you're beautiful. You will spread your wings and fly.

We live in a society where we envy others without knowing what they went through to reach success. We must learn how to invest in ourselves and tap into our God-given gifts. We all have unique gifts. What's your gift? Ask the holy spirit to give you discernment.

Jumpstart

Taxes is a jumpstart for the business ventures that I want to expand into. Taxes as a vehicle will engage you about 3 to 4 months out of the year. You can leverage the extra time to move into other areas you are interested in. Making the vision your own keeps you moving forward rather than looking around at what others are doing.

Everything hinges upon perception. Everyone can bring their vision to life, but we must wholeheartedly believe that vision. At your job, begin to perfect what you have learned and gone beyond; you show yourself your capabilities. You now know your capability. Once you perfect, you can expand. If your job is not rewarding you for your capability, you now have the confidence to move out of that space and excel elsewhere.

I knew that I was one of the best employees on the floor at the biotech firm I worked at. Companies may desire those workers, but they must build in the mechanisms to support and reward that initiative. Unfortunately, some firms hold individuals back from their potential.

The Taxing of Ke'sha Dennis

They set the bar as maintaining the status quo through the mechanisms they support. Your adherence to that mentality keeps you stuck. Once you change your mentality, you must make a move. You can no longer remain in that stuck space. Either change your mindset, which will eventually change what you are doing or stay there and get left behind.

Too many are stuck on job security rather than financial security. They have not connected with the truth of what they are working toward. Retirement is not what you are working toward. We should all be working toward a life of financial freedom. I see 70 years old women who are still working because they have to. They don't have the financial freedom to live the life they deserve. These events have reshaped my way of thinking about finances. My goal is not to work past the age of 55.

Ke'sha Dennis

Chapter 11: Out of My Control

Eye of the Storm

I realized that attempting to do things myself was problematic. When I let God take the wheel, everything worked out every time. We as people don't fix anything. God fixes. I had to learn to stop getting in my own way.

Losing control, you can still be safe and secure: comfortable while being uncomfortable. I had to burn sage and pray for many days. It is the quietness in the eye of the storm. A lot of craziness can be going on around you, but if you sit still and get quiet, you can get the lesson of the moment. I now ask the Holy Spirit for discernment, and the answer is always revealed. God is always in control, and there's a different kind of comfort, that comes with that.

Remove yourself from the chaos and look at it from a different point of view. That's when the epiphanies happen. I didn't feel the transformation God put me through in that moment. I have since learned the eye of the storm as a transmutation. I was the person that was always talking and moving. When you don't learn it this way, God's going to show you his way.

I talk to women and always ask what lesson did you learn during your breakthrough? You look for the lesson and the silver lining. That's where the growth occurs. Many don't find their peace because they don't view the situation as a lesson. They feel like the victim and play that role in most aspects of life. You think that it is because people don't love or respect you, but the truth is that you don't love yourself. If you loved yourself, you would demand love from others. Those who refuse to take accountability for their own lives will never grow.

My experience is that when I get the lesson, I immediately get the blessing. The moment I am grateful is the moment I grow. I almost feel guilty for figuring it out. You get blessings that you may not feel that you deserve. They come back to back. They come right on time.

Loving Yourself

When I walked up the stairs and couldn't breathe, that was the first time that I saw myself for who I was at that time. I was 310lbs. I saw myself and knew I needed to change, so I did something about it. When you are dealing with a history of abuse and mistreatment, you may need therapy. But other than that, almost everything is mental. You must push the mind-reset button. You must see yourself authentically. Get back to loving yourself and doing what you love to do. You must figure out what works for you. Connect with your desires.

The problem with society is that they want you to do things one way. If you don't want to do it that way or if that doesn't work for you, find another way. We don't have to fit into societies norm. The goal is the results. If you can't figure it out, get help. You must honestly commit to taking the time out for you. Nothing will change if you don't do your part. Stop making excuses and get active.

Time management is critical to this commitment. You must make time for you. If you must wake up a half-hour earlier to have time for yourself, do that. You must change your mentality. When I saw myself at that weight, I didn't know who that person was. I needed to find the real Ke'sha under my fat suit.

I know there is another chick out there that is living with blinders on. She is walking around with her view of herself that is based on the last time she connected with herself. She may have gained weight from having kids like me. She may have lost herself in marriage. She may be working to chauffeur kids around instead of taking care of self. Sometimes, you must stop and see yourself. You must connect with what you are right now and reconnect with who you know yourself to be authentically. When you see that difference, you must change.

It's like a child throwing a tantrum then recognizing that everyone is looking. They get up from the floor and feel embarrassed. That was me. I was unhealthy. I needed to change that. But first, I had to see myself. Who are you authentically?

Coming Back

My mom gave me the greatest gift. She put the Bible, the foundation of God in my hand. When the seed is planted, you will always go back.

Life is all lessons. I have learned to:

Take time for me. I had to learn that I am no good for anyone if I'm not good to myself. I found myself irritated and not happy. I was not taking the time to love on me. Who can love me better than me? I realized I wasn't feeling loved, because I didn't love myself.

Say no more often. I say no for the heck of it sometimes. I have fun with No sometimes. I want to say yes and say no some because I can. I learned to say no to reclaim my time. I found another piece of the puzzle of life. I have time for myself because I learned to say no.

You will get what you pray for within His will. I asked God to expose everyone who was not for me. My circle is down to a dot. Those who have fallen away were those who were draining my energy and my time. Unfortunately, when you're advancing in life; those around you become envious. Their inferiority and inability to accomplish what you have, creates the green envy monster. Once God exposes these people, steer clear if you want success.

Patience. I must have the patience to be still. Not doing anything has always been a struggle for me. To sit within my thoughts is a new practice. I used to be impatient to the point where I could not sit for too long. I had to be doing something. Cooking, reading, vision boards, or something. Sitting still is priceless now that I understand the power of being still. I still find it difficult at times, but I'm aware when I need to take a moment. I unplug myself from the matrix. It doesn't matter what is going on around me. I unplug. I gain peace, tranquility, calmness, serenity, gratitude and love. I gain a clearer head—a mental reset. At this point, I take it whenever I need it. It's mandatory.

Forgiveness. Many people feel that if you forgive someone, you must continue to deal with the person. I have a different point of view. I feel that you could forgive someone from a distance. You can pray from a distance. Their spirit may not align with yours. I am big on energy. If your energy is so negative that it drains mine, I must separate myself from you. Forgiveness is letting go of anger and resentment. You can send them positive energy and thoughts, but you are not obligated or pressured to spend time with them. You don't have to be the receptor for everyone's energy. We all don't have to be attached. You can love and care without intentionally accepting incongruent energy.

If you love, love enough to let it go. As women, we use the word love too loosely. When we are in love, we feel the need to be attached and obligated. I have kids by them, so I'm obligated. I know they don't have a place to go, so I feel obligated. Until we realize that we don't owe anybody anything, we will continue to say yes. As bad as it may feel to say no, you must love it enough to let it go. If it is not contributing to your progress, it is taking away from your progress. Some people come into your life for seasons. They are for a reason or a lifetime. You may think that they are the lifetime, but that's not the way God sees it. If someone is continually hurting or using you, let them go. If God wants a relationship to prosper, he'll provide the tools for it to work.

Be careful what you pray for. When I prayed for God to remove people, they left. They were ghosts. He exposed them in ways that allowed me to see them for who they are. Even if they changed, I saw the truth so clearly that I know not to give them another chance with me.

You must really adjust your mindset to comprehend yourself authentically. When you live the truth of who you are, you attract what is like you. You must trust the process of the attraction that comes with authentic living. It's a cool, rollercoaster ride. Life feels dangerous. Some laugh, cry and startle, but by the end, you can't wait to do it again.

Chapter 12: The Come Up

Within two years, I went from 2 to 94 employees. I made my previous yearly wage in just over two weeks. I advertised a position within my company and received 236 applicants. I opened the new tax season with over 7500 leads. I owe all this success to my understanding of Yeshua, myself, and my vision.

The Journey

Yeshua was more specific than a form of godliness. The understanding of the role of Yeshua as a guide and pilot while I learn, and follow is critical to the process. Yeshua in the context of the holy trinity is more than just a notion of an infallible god-man. Yeshua is an example of being connected and led by divine providence.

Many people express an understanding of themselves and a list of the things they would like to change about themselves. What I have learned is that I can integrate the best qualities of myself. I can submit them back to Yeshua in humility and a desire to learn. The result may not be what I intended or expected, but I submit to being led. I am comfortable with evolving daily.

I have a vision of the company. I know where it's going and what I want it to do. Alone, I developed what I wanted. I put that into the atmosphere and began to connect with people, resources, and realities. I thought and had to move. I willed it to come to life. I had the determination to make it happen. I learned and continue to learn. I found a marketer that markets well for me. She caught my attention with her wording. I brought her on board. She taught me how to brand myself for the business. The marketing worked. People began to connect with me. My CFO found me, came into my office one day and sat down confidently. She told me that she had been following me on Facebook for a while. That was surprising to me. It was another of those moments when the calling stared me in the face. I have come to expect those connections now. I can rest in the knowledge that if we are meant to work together, the connection will be effortless and never forced.

I am building relationships with people that connect with me and are like-minded. My vision is coming to fruition like Superman fast. It's been six years since I put on my vision board to start a new business. That board is completed. It is time to put together the next board. What I envision happens within five years or less.

The Start-Up

My latest endeavor is Lady Buzz. Many black women needed to exchange and network. I started in March. In 4 months, the group grew to 4000 women. I am creating a network of opportunity for so many that need another form of passive income. I know that I need to reach those people. I found a reliance on technology that I had not experienced before.

God already had a gift on the other side of my experience. How do you get there is the question? You must be willing and ready to make the change from the guilt and shame that may have become comfortable.

It reminds me of my complacency while I was 310 pounds. When I was big, I was treated differently. Your challenge is to define your identity to align with your vision. You could walk up to a person, offer help, and be rebuffed because they don't think they need the help. I was the one who wished people could have told the truth. No one said anything. When I realized, I talked to my family and asked, "Why didn't you tell me?"

The Taxing of Ke'sha Dennis

"We thought you knew!" and I didn't. Even if they had brought my weight to my attention, I would not have realized it and made changes until it resonated with me. Until I looked in the mirror and examined myself, until I made the comparison with what I WANTED—a vision for myself, the identity I desired for myself, I was not going to be motivated to make a change. And in that way, it's not about motivation, but rather inspiration. You must be inspired to see something different for yourself. You must be excited about becoming. That is your first step.

I started my come-up by viewing motivational speakers. First, it was an inspiration toward something new and structured. Next, I was putting the pieces of the puzzle together. I noticed their platforms and strategies. I noticed their multiple streams of income. They sold books, courses, speaking engagements, and subscriptions. I structured my sell, my value add, and my target. My sell is taxes. My value add is to return time to people that I work with. My target are people who want to run business, not run after their financials.

I became an evangelist of sort and told people about my new friends. They are my audible book friends. I have them available at a moment's notice to provide insight, advice, or perspective. Rich Dad Poor Dad is my favorite. I can relate. If I had the rich dad perspective earlier on, my life would have been different. My come up would have accelerated.

The transformation to the come up is a brain training experience. We are not typically prepared for the identity definition and the brain shift that must occur. Your daily activities are about work, but they are mostly about managing the mind. That how I lost the weight. That's how I built the business. That's how I'm manifesting now.

Creating Opportunities and Income

My goal is to help all my cousins win. To see them happier, healthier, and more whole. Mentally, they are still thinking like a fat person. They don't see that they need to change. It will not be enough to tell them about a change. They must be awakened to their calling. The best mirror you can hold up is your own success. The best contribution you can make is to make the process available for them when they are ready to listen. And the process is mental. Until you change the mind, you can't move forward.

People walk past each other without a real connection. Not knowing your people or your tribe has cost many their success. I have also witnessed true love operating in groups of people. They embrace each other. They take up for each other. I have witnessed a whole team leave because one of their team members was mistreated. We must return to that reality of love. We must find that tribe of belonging. The search begins with a clear identification of You, your identity.

I started thinking differently about trying to help. Now, I place my money into me. I am going to another level, and that will draw a new crowd. I was trying to make them me. They are not me. At first, I felt like Yeshua. "I'm telling you how to get there, and you're not getting it." Then, they're mad at you because you have it and they don't. That's how you know you are succeeding. He dusted off and kept it moving. That's what I have learned to do.

Relationships. Some of your greatest limiters, haters, and laggards will be your family members. It may even be your mom. You must change your perspective away from childhood relationships to adult relationships, asking about fitness, influence, and progress in relationships.

Generosity. Our perception of being more like God is giving freely. You need to charge for the value you provide. This is Business. You give a break to certain people but not everybody.

Opportunities. There are too many ways to make money out there. Whatever you have going on, look for passive income. Find ways to make money in the beginning. Find ways for that money to make money at the next opportunity. At the third level, find ways that the money made can leverage additional money that can work to make money.

Talents. I believe that we all have talent. Tap into that talent. If you yodel, get on television and yodel. If you are a seamstress, make unique clothing. Start an online boutique. Everyone is online. You don't even have to leave the comfort of your home. Online businesses are available for little money down.

Investment. Women say that they don't have money. If you have on shoes, your hair done, and nails done, Yes you do. Start with sacrifice. There's a course online that costs $99. If you can't hold on to that money, you have a deeper problem. Invest in classes to learn another way.

Equipment. If you can't invest in yourself, you must explore what is keeping you from doing that. You can find a cheap laptop for $300. Start saving. They even have Go Fund Me. Ask your friends, family, and anyone else to invest in the start-up of your business. Offer them a shout out or a byline or an equity share. Find out what your options are. Even if you don't have access to finances, you must leverage the people, information, and time that you do have.